WORKS AND DAYS
and other poems

Works and Days
and other poems

IRVING FELDMAN

An Atlantic Monthly Press Book
LITTLE, BROWN AND COMPANY
Boston   Toronto

ATLANTIC-LITTLE, BROWN BOOKS

ARE PUBLISHED BY
LITTLE, BROWN AND COMPANY
IN ASSOCIATION WITH
THE ATLANTIC MONTHLY PRESS

PUBLISHED SIMULTANEOUSLY IN CANADA
BY LITTLE, BROWN & COMPANY (CANADA)
LIMITED

PRINTED IN HOLLAND

Some of these poems first appeared in the following:

*Atlantic, Carleton Miscellany, castalia, Commentary, Harper's
Bazaar, Kenyon Review, Midstream, The Nation, New Mexico
Quarterly, New Republic, New World Writing, Noble Savage,
Noonday, Partisan Review, Poetry, Portfolio and Art News
Journal, The Saturday Review,* and *Western Review.* "Lullaby to
Two Growing Old" appeared originally in *The New Yorker.*

To my father and mother

I

II Works and Days/33

III

I

THE SAINT

God, you were the handle to every door
And I walked the world unlocking them
To find always myself. I see the poor
And starve, the naked are my shame,
The evil undo, the sick burn
Me, the wretched are my sorrow.
I never wanted this — so to be torn
By the plow of pity in every furrow.

I wanted only to be there,
And be still and slowly to grow
Empty and round, to be all in my ear
And listen for your endless Now.

But this goodness gives me away from you,
For love has scattered my soul through
Fields and towns. I rise like grass
Against myself, so thick I cannot pass
To you till I wither in every part.
O God, I would have been your hollow gulf!
Why did you put your dam across my heart
To overwhelm me with myself!

11

THE PROPHET

I am your stone. I seek the center.
Lean back, bend over, I know one way.
You cannot move. I weigh. I weigh.
I am your doom. Your city shall not burn.
The flood has gone by, the fever passed.
Get home. Empty the square
As your hearts are empty. Only I am there.
Everywhere. I bring all things down.

Your eyes wander to the ground.
You yearn for density, the solid,
You want blocks, you want the harder stone:
Clay will not do; granite, not marble.
Your souls crave no room. All is brought together.
You shall be as stone and wedge yourselves down.
Where all things are one.

AFTER THE JUDGMENT

(A god speaks to his city)

As a mother does, I draw my day of doom
Like a blanket gently from your heads,
While you lie frightened in the womb
Where still you stretch and feel for death.

You hardly know what you have done. What had been
Your greatest terror you now desire
Alone, for this is being born again:
To be for the first time all that you were.

You'd thought your little fears were the footfalls
Of a god upon your hearts, and prayed
A tiny doom to close over your souls
Like an eye's blink. But still you were afraid,

Afraid that darkness was unreal as light;
Had cried for more and on your heads had drawn
The days of your lives to make your night:
In doom you found only your dawn.

So dark with despair, you could not know
The day I had made. I refused no prayer:
As if what I should do could overthrow
The destiny you bear! to be as you are.

To live was always to be judged, and what
Was hardest: to be judged as right. For all things
Are so, even you. And now you cannot
Hide from the sunlight of your beings.

Then lift your heads and see how I have knit
My coverlet of doom beyond your praise.
I have cast over you your light
And wrapped you in the innocence of days.

THE DEATH OF VITELLOZZO VITELLI *

Vitelli rides west toward Fano, the morning sun
Has spread his shadow before him, his head is cast
Upon the road beyond the horse, and now in vain

He works his spurs and whip. For all his speed, his past
Like a heavy wind has thrown his death far before
Him, and not till midday shall he fill the waste

Of light he has made with the goldness of his spur
And the greenness of his cape. Then shall he stand
At last by the bridge at Fano and know no more

His way than the farmer at noon who looks from his land
To his heart and knows not where next to turn his plow;
Or lovers who have stayed abed and reach a hand

And yet have turned away, even as they do so,
To move their legs and sigh, wearied of their embrace
— Yet nothing else seems worth their while. His road shall go

Before him, having broken itself in two ways:
One goes to Borgia in Fano, and one toward Rome.
But his shadow hurries from his feet to his face.

* *Murdered by Cesare Borgia in 1502.*

IMAGINARY FIGURE OF SAMSON WITH PILLARS

TO M. D. FELD

He seems, though straining, almost in repose,
So smooth the grooves of his beard, his head half-turned
Aside, his eyes about to close.
Ambiguously, his hands are laid upon
The stones. Is it strenuous rest? or does
He press them out? or brace their falling in?

And why are not his feet upon the ground,
But wedged against the columns? as though he had
Leaped and only here had caught his bound.
Why is the temple unceiled? why are the proud
Pillars half-finished or ruined? And where's
The drunk idolatrous crowd?

Samson, my image, here I alone
Come to adore, knowing how, self-sculpted,
You struck your warrior will into this stone,
Where, still struggling, it bears the world apart:
As if, keystone-wise, you meant all opposites
To war within your bursting, concretive heart.

O, if self-begotten be self-undone,
And better to fall among the evil
Than turn to stone standing alone,
I come to worship though you cannot save.
Overhead, the sky abides revolving
What peace it has, and underfoot, the grave.

Here you stand with glorious might
Joining and disjoining in your loins and chest
This barren temple with heroic spite.

In whose great hand is my hand laid?
My heart is overreached, my path
With a moving mist is overlaid.
I wander in this evil breath
That glides on stones and, stooping, sulks.
Is this sullen stumbling faith?
Joyless and ashen as one who stalks
His shadow I go, and do not know
If I am but His staff Who walks.

God, You bring me on the hill,
And here in many-faced mist
Am I misled and wander still,
Even to my death. My heart, like a fist,
Is bound upon itself to beat
The swirling faces of the past
Till all their mouths shall speak my fate.
O this I will, yet never feel
Your path singing in my feet.

Remember that once my face shone!
Now how shall Your rod strike a brook
Out of my heart's heavy stone!
Did I not the golden calf unmake?
Did I not Your word impart?
Then have You blotted me from Your book
That I vanish on this page apart?
Hear me! though I can but speak
With cloven tongue and quartered heart.

Not so. Not so. You overbear
Even my fear. Here lies asleep
In the palm of my heart as in my ear
Your word; if I mutter and creep,
Feet and tongue are mine, and this eye
That wept. You speak and hear and keep
My hand, and though myself I deny,
You are no God of sticks: now in light
You burst from the mist and are my destiny.

Face on face shine in Your face.
Path on path run in Your face.
This path is the promised place. I die.

PROMETHEUS

Nailed to his Caucasian loneliness,
A thousand years he stands. The mountains drive
Their storm of stone. And no one comes. No one.
Not, as once, the eagle ever and again,
Not Io lowing through the meadow of the world,
Nor the tender daughters of Ocean, nor the suave
God of the waters. Only this loneliness
Going blue in the gorges of his eyes.

The sap-soaked wood cries against the axe's mouth,
The apple screams into Eve the notes
Of the generations' hubbub. But who spoke
To the mouth of his solitude? God had forgotten,
And slept beyond his cloud-filled eyes.
But Prometheus stands on, of all things the worst:
To be a victim and have no torturer.
He must speak — where is there ear?
He must hear — where is a voice? And who
Shall bear grapes to the winery of his bones?
The rising vine is broken: arm speaks against
Arm, heart rivals beat with beat, lip
Utters itself to lip; solitude's
A raging breath spoken within. His body
Is dialectic, war, voices.

Confabulation of winds. Autumn dusk,
Blue laid upon blue flowing in his throat.
And the mountains riding into deep shadows.
(And he would be with the gods again,
Leaping to the chase, his great arm raised,
And glory, wild and eloquent as silver,
Pouring from the pan of his loins.
But the taste of doom is on his tongue; its iron pang
Taints the immensity of his body:
Alone, and nailed through the heart into nature.)
The wind arising tears out the infant voice
Still curled unborn in Prometheus' ear;

The rising winter tears the vine, and driven
On the blue, leaves cry aloud
Reaching along the alleys of his body —
To fumble, mutter, depart.
And godliness perishes with the vine.
Now Adam and Eve wander from his heart,
Arm murders arm, fouling the late leaves
With blood; the furrows sputter sand. And the wind
Whirls the dying upon the dead — centuries, centuries —
Till the shifting babel of the leaves builds
Its word to the tongue of Prometheus; he speaks.

'O mountain, mother of iron, sink into me.
Let iron beget iron, that from this iron root
I flower iron. The god shall wake and return;
And though I sing only as the anvil sings,
I shall din upon his ear till
The white hammer of the heavenly voice
Strikes itself to rainbow against me. He returns —
And yet shall creep through my veins to pray my heart!'

CATO DYING

Indifferent, in this torchlit dark, the restless noise . . .
Of sentries' sharp call, servants' tread,
His son's voice, sinking; they cannot cross
The room to him, nothing can exceed
This space. And so had it been his life long.
Not Cato had he made, but emptiness
He had carved about him. The world was wrong,
And only in this silence was there peace.

Dimly he lifts his head and leaning forward
Sees on the couch his body going away.
Would it leave! that now at last his sword
Gives Cato to himself. Stay, stay!
Circumstance gropes everywhere, and flits
Upon the world kindling its harsh whisper.
See where the torch, guttering, impatiently sits
With round arms folding darkness in its fire!

A door is opened from their dark room to his.
Had his friends heard? They would come near, and yet
Are trammeled in the torch; their faces are blood-rose
And crossed by shadows which, like whispers, net.
He throws the petalled sword among the rose-heads,
Disdainfully: even here the world was not
Good. The whispers still, the roses have fled,
With his own hands he turns himself inside out.

This joyous space he feels is everywhere,
And yet a point within his chest, and yet beyond
These friends, beyond even the Caesar who hurries here;
So great it is they cannot comprehend.
And he alone knows that Cato is no more:
For nothing now is not the space that Cato is.
The torch is turning petals into rose,
And long, long its tongues speak in his ear.

LOSS

FOR I. B.

The world gathers itself away from her,
As a robe fold on fold from the hand is struck,
And slowly lays itself with care upon
The horizon — as mountain, tree, rock.

As in a distance, it would put itself away.
A mother it had given, a mother took.
And now a lover and a son dumbly
Compose themselves — as mountain, tree, and rock.

Across a desert, she and the mountains stare.
She sees the snow, the burning green, and thinks, My dust.
Their golden veins gaze back and do not know
How now she holds their emptiness in trust.

Nor how they drive their glory along the sky
Because they suck the nothing in her breast.
Who stands unshivering in the absence of all
Gives gold to the root and goats to the crest.

Should summer wind the swallow, bell, and orange
Bring to her on its blue open hand,
She will not take; there is no having back.
Her nothing she gives. And so shall stand.

NON-BEING

And all about him rock — with heavy greyness as of a sigh.
And yet Prometheus saw at once the sardonic humor of the place,
How the mountains tilted back their heads against the sky
And twisted out a smile; something similar passed on his face.

After a thousand years he thought he saw the joke,
And began, almost nostalgically, to giggle; even his joints
Felt a certain lightness, it took so little to provoke
A knee, merely, say, the wryness of two opposing points.

Another aeon passed and he laughed outright;
He felt himself, in fact, the universal satirist,
The final glittering of the rictus of cosmic spite.
Then nothing really mattered — and his mirth bubbled away in a
                                                  [mist.

What terrible cackle bounds blatant through the vale?
O come to the mountain and see a suit of clothes on a nail!

FLOOD

TO LIONEL TRILLING

The first day it rained we were glad.
How could we know? The heavy air
Had lain about us like a scarf, though work
Got done. Everything seemed easier.
In the streets a little mud.

With the first faint drops, a tiny breeze
Trembled the cornsilk, and the frailest leaves
Turned on their stems this way and that.
Coming from the fields for lunch
I thought it my sweat.

On the second day streamlets ran
In the furrows; the plow stuck,
The oxen balked. On the third day
The rain ran from the roof like a sea.
I thought I would visit town.

Farmers from their farms, merchants from stores,
Laborers, we filled the town. I
Stayed with a cousin. We were told
The granary was full, we could live
A thousand days should the river rise impetuously.

The fifth day the clouds seemed hung
From the tops of the tallest trees. The sun
We did not see at all. And the rain
Beat down as if to crush the roof.
I did not shave or write my wife.

On the sixth day, we moved the women
And children to the town church, built
On the highest ground hard by the granary.
We finished work on the levee.
The river was thick with silt.

A dark drizzle started in my head.
Next day it trickled on the walls of my skull
Like black earth drifting down a grave.
We resolved to stay in the church come what will.
That day I did not leave my bed.

From where the rain? and why on us?
Not even the wisest knows or dares guess.
Did we not plan, care, save, toil,
Did we lay idle or lust, did we waste or spoil?
Therefore, why on us?

The husbandman from his flock,
Husband from wife, the miser from his heap,
The wise man from his wit, from her urn
The widow — are tumbled all, as a man might knock
The ashes from his pipe.

And the days descended in a stream,
So fast they could not be told apart.
In the church all went black.
Once I lay with Lenah as in a dream.
Another time I found myself at Adah's back.

If no one gets up at dawn to wind
The clock, shall not the state run down?
If no one gets up to go to the fields
To feed the cows, to sow the wheat,
To reap, how shall the state grow fat?

One comes telling us Noah has built a boat
That through the flood he may ride about,
And filled it all with animals.
Just like the drunken fool, that slut-
Chaser, to think of no one else.

I feed my friends and kin; twenty-nine thrived
In my home. But mad Noah harangues the air
Or goes muttering in his cuff
As though a god were up his sleeve.
Who is Noah to get saved?

I am a farmer, I love my wife,
My sons are many and strong, my land is green.
This is my cousin, he lives in town,
An honest man, he rises at dawn.
We were children together.

Shall not the world run down?
Why on us? Did we not plan?
Does not black blood flow before my eyes
And blackness brim inside my skull?
Did we lie idle? Did we spoil?

Out of its harness the mind wild as a horse
Roams the rooms and streets. There are some that say
Noah sits amid the rude beasts in his ark
And they feed one upon the other in the dark
And in the dark they mate. And some say worse:

That a griffin was born, and centaur
And sphinx hammer at the door.
Groans and moans are heard, by some the roar
Of giant Hippogriff. Still others cry
That all about the earth is dry!

Dry as if no rain had fallen,
As if we were not awaiting the swollen
River, as if the clouds did not sit
On our chimneys, or the waters
Tumble past our windows in spate.

And some here say a dove has come,
Sure, they think, the sign of a god.
And others say that Noah walks the street
Puffed with news. But bid him wait!
We are busy with our flood.

SAINT AND LEPER

I

No penance brought me peace or good; those chains,
That hermit silence, all emptiness of sense
Had but led me to the heart's wild land,
Betrayed — for there too I fed: those are shadowy pains
Wherein lurks the shadow of one's hand.

None may raise a hand but in self-indulgence;
I murdered awe with my starving trance,
And the shrinking world withdrew, became mine;
All coming affliction yielded to my omniscient glance
— Self-denial is the self's strongest wine.

And on the desert's liquid airs my delight
Arose dancing, drunk with its appetite
For shadow, pure shadow, shadow and air.
O golden city, I watched it mount beyond sight,
Still burned through by my desert despair.

II

And then a leper came, wearing his flesh
Like a rag, ancient sores parched to ash,
With rotting hands embraced me where I stood,
And drawing me to the circle of his moving trash,
Whispered, 'Saint, thou shalt yet be good.'

The horror of that mouth, that slime-smeared bone!
And yet I leaned and kissed his lips with my own,
Till from their fallow clay an apple tree
Burst forth and shone. And then my voice's leprous moan
I heard cry out, 'Leper, I am thee!'

Exchanging natures, we whirled around that tree:
The leper odious there in my glory,
His sore my purity. All creation's trials
We danced, evil that brings the good to reality,
Thus bowed together — lips of One who smiles.

ON THE EVE: A MARTYR DREAMS

I who of all women of God
Was fruitless, useless; I who crept
Like a wind through children leaves I could not nod;
I who untouched sat and slept
On boughs, in caves, an empty wind
That could not suckle fields, although it wept;
I who was nothing, not evil, not kind,
Now that you sin, am like an apple,
So pressed with love to the rind.

This day the flames have come like dogs
To tear and bear away my flesh,
But in their jaws I laugh like spring in logs.
The hounds of flame now wag and stretch
To greet the maid who comes to wed,
And now your wives conceive in me by ash.
You shall not find me with the dead,
Having mothered your sins and fires
At dawn I arise from your bed.

A SPEECH BY ABRAHAM

Here have I come with Isaac my only son,
Three days riding toward Moriah here.
Over the rocks the asses scrambled
And the sand and weeds, and the drivers
Cursing and urging, and myself, and young
Isaac racing the bounding rabbits,
Stoning the sky-drunk birds, the stones
Mounting quickly to them, or curving off.
Darling son, so long awaited! Lean
And dewy and blackhaired, black hair wetly
Hanging over th' eyes, wild and wet, mouth awater,
And skin glistening. And the avid body
Long-muscled, crouching, running, the wrist snapped
Sharply and the stone's away flying.
And the bird's caught dead and drops lying
Soft on the rocks.
        O my sky-drunk child, so must I catch you!
— Where your heart's aflutter like the thrush
Racing in its windy heaven of chest,
Drunk on the sweet rushing air. And soft
You'll lie on the altar, and soon with God.
For now is the spring and the rivers flow
Mightily down, curling over the rim,
Flood the plain, carrying all away.
And the Lord came to me in a dream;
Three magical angels, bright and sweet, yet
Awful, the central one saying, Offer
Up to me Isaac as burnt sacrifice
On a mountain in Moriah.
        So we've come, the asses wood-laden,
Picking their way over the rocks and sand,
The drivers urging them, myself leading
Yet drawn forward, trembling, eyes fallen back,
Drymouthed, and my son running
Through the bushes like a hare.

THE WIDOW

As when a god's possessed a bush
And for a second blazes there
To seize the lonely traveler's stare,
And then is gone in a swirling rush;

Startled, he looks around, and sees
His steadfast day has turned a night
Blooming after-images of light,
And he is lost and on his knees:

So, like a black god-blasted tree,
She stood beside herself, a double-
Image, consumed, banished, awful,
Dark and bright with agony;

Stood, and her dazzling face was freed,
Whirled its whitened leaf before me.
I am falling. I cannot see —
My burden heaving, my path in weed.

THE OLD MEN

Ho! Persephone brings flowers, to them
New styles in spring. In seven glittering
Greys, under round grey hats of straw
— Lo! to the fifing sun's tune
The old men come on, stride, march,
Drill, straight as the ties of lovers!
(And their bones have drawn together
In gentle communities of joints,
Like weary soldiers dreaming head to head.)

Hup, they go, ho! in grey jackets,
Grey shoes, sleek as boys, smiling,
Striding on, the gay granite legions,
Persephone's grooms, all together, raise
Chins, link arms, step out, hiking, marching,
Down down into the earth!

II

WORKS AND DAYS

TO FERNANDO

My name is Laughter, and I laughed
Knowing everything's absurd.
For God in his ironic craft
Made all more and less than his word.

And the fool world dances on the spit
Of my tongue — whirling, leaping, crying
Delight within my fiery wit!
And I laugh all the while I am dying.

1. THE ARK

Ghetto-born, depression-bred,
Squeezed between the finger and thumb
Of Famine and traditional Dread,
I learned all history's a *pogrom*.

Scared tutelage of the dead.
The hand that strokes the silken shawl,
I learned, may not strike red.
A Jew's defense, the Wailing Wall.

Learned to be patient under blows,
Suspect the world, yet ready to be
Wiped across my neighbor's nose,
Chided then for being filthy.

Learned the cost of life in cents,
To measure every ring and rag.
Saw Israel's shining tents
Fold up like a doctor's bag.

Learned the little-bourgeois ruse;
To save the day against the night,
And night for day, then lose
Them both, worrying if I were right.

Free of the flood, our ghetto tied
Smugly to the rope of His wrath,
We thought to put the world aside
Like the dirty ring after a bath.

*

The fog in curtains under the lamps,
Kitchen vapors on the pane,
Smoke puffing out with cramps,
Distant gossip in the drain.

Furniture that I recall:
Solemn lumbar embassy,
Plump and bowing from the wall
To whisper, Comfort's ecstasy.

Sleep! those lotus-eaters said,
A conspiracy in the bowels restores
The interlocking trust of bread.
Sleep alone never bores.

A liver lounging in a pot;
Mama boiling the kitchen runes.
Always I see her face a blot
In the sacred oval of the spoons.

Grey and sweet and shining eyes,
Freckled arms that took with ardor
The scalds and bundles of sacrifice
— To fill again love's larder.

She kneeled to dust the furniture,
But rose with an abstracted eye.
What was it she had seen there?
In spite of all, people die.

In spite of every daily care,
The wash, the rent, sickness, meals,
The building of a life is air,
For death is something else.

The pot grew cool by afternoon
And wore a smiling beard of tears.
A drop crawled drowsily down,
And fell, like the falling years.

The radiator knocked like a ghost,
Outside, the wind and bawling cats.
My father nodded at his post,
Messiah thundered fireside chats.

Papa — shy, sour, slow —
Enduring the worried years like a stone,
Falling, falling asleep over the radio,
Dreaming of his son.

That all proclaimed the quotidian,
And should the day ache with glory,
Prescribed a little medicine.
Grandeurs of our infirmity.

Fed up with the narrow pot,
Every day I ate disgust.
Dishes, death, closet of rot,
Who invented this can of dust!

Well, I flew away from all that —
The old rock, the old ark
Hung aloft on Ararat —
Crow lost in a world of wrack.

2. WRACK

A lonely music arose and bid
Me follow. And I went.
Under the night's unwaking lid
I learned what dying meant.

And took upon me mourner's weed
And ashes of a fallen son,
Thinking Esau's desert seed
Was happier than my own,

And being choked with memory
I might thereby blot out my name,
Thought breath came best in beggary.
Alas! it was all the same.

With orphan girls I slept it off,
My patrimony of dust.
Hammered down the nights like a cough:
Ghetto contempt, ghetto distrust.

Wintered, paltry, threadbare things,
I took their nakedness to wrap
My fatted calf — Isaac of strings
And straw, curtains of blue burlap.

Ah, those tenement pastorals,
Dressed in the rags of love and such,
Shepherding little animals
Who asked for nothing needing too much.

      *   *   *

Her sweat, mascara, breasts implied
The wherewithal to float an affair,
And to her poverty testified
A certain lankness, pallor of hair.

At dawn her eyes opened wide,
Like doors on an empty hall, the stair,
The street's cold light — till I was outside,
And doubting I had been there.

*   *   *

Along the street a winter wind
Rattled its elementary war.
Breathless armies arrived and grinned,
Entered their trench by a subway door.
Leaflets from trees proclaimed the end.
And the wind came on as before.

Crow

— after Corbière

Uneasy and restless everywhere
Arrogant as a wild hair.

A Jew among *goyim,* but not with Jews
Rolling stone, in his own shoes.

When out of love, wanting to be in
Loved, now impatient of women.

To strangers pleasant and to friends unkind
Hare with dogs, dog to the hind.

His life a stick with which to beat — his life
Poetry to tell that strife.

Improper with the good, faithful son
Probity is his perversion.

And bad conscience too for all the bother
Of dealing father's justice to father.

His code of honor: Mock everyone
Being a mourner in the sun.

Remembers Lethe, otherwise forgetful
Heaven-bound desiring hell.

He chokes with himself when taking the air
Always out, at home nowhere.

And goes to sleep chewing on his breath
Wakes again to think of death.

Politics

*Tant vaut le métier
tant vaut l'homme.* — Diderot.

Of love we planned the total reign,
Yet could not bear each other's words.
Our mutual and the world's disdain
Were all the glue that held our shards.

Too ambitious to be at ease
And too honorable for lies,
Our talents turning our disease,
We festered with the public flies.

Our avid youthful powers would live
Without the common daily sop.
The world held up its leviathan sieve,
The duller ones got caught in a job.

As for the rest, our mockery
Betrayed us out of plumb and measure:
Our trade became idiosyncrasy,
Our program but a little pleasure.

And so we built our politics
Upon the air, like Israelites
With straw who could not fashion bricks.
Condemning duties, what good were rights!

Yet what is it Leviathan allots?
— Bureaucracy or violence,
His stomach or his teeth. Poor prophets
Of love, we chose the desert, and Jonah's hollow melon.

Forgetting

What was I at twenty? there
In the city streets, winding frown
Of the twilit beast of stone, where
The bodies of youths were drizzling down.

What was I then? I forget.
The falling mystery of my breath
Stands in eyeless walls of regret.
City, incarnation of death!

I sit amid my mortal rain.
Although like Theseus I fought,
I have become what I have slain.

My lamp is glowing red and grave.
But darkness is a greater thought
And seeks me through the cave.

Melancholy

The wind tore the sky to tatters
Above the stone bridges of the Seine,
That winter day, the driven rain
Leaned down in long ladders.

And my eye, suspended between
The promised power, the murdered form,
Beheld the luxury of storm,
The pathos of the sighing scene.

Wind, through shreds of greyness scream
And crack the saucers of the stream!
I could not fall, could not rise.

The thought of death, the wind's sieve,
Gathered all I could not live
And all the rest shook down in cries.

Division

The world is parted where I pursue
The horizon's river in its flight.
And now its sadness like a night
Is darkening the brown, the blue.

Such a line a child might tie
Across the whiteness of a plane,
And then with godly paint ordain:
Let this be earth, let this be sky.

For me, the line I cannot cross.
In exile, mourning I endure
Every dying, every loss.

My eye runs on! my heart clings.
I wait upon the blackened shore,
Remembering the time of kings.

Apocalypse

At the end of Forty-second Street
A broken sun goes down in squalls.
The wind-bewildered twilight
Is blasted on the cracking walls.

The bells begin, against the stone
They butt their swollen volumes of doom,
The auto horns cry out, Atone! —
From their jobs the poor go crowding home.

Ragged glory of the day's
Dying; winter riots on the drum,
Summoning the poor to their patience.
Salvation is a growing numb.

The bells are pounding the last glint.
Where Seventh Avenue makes a cross,
Grazing on the shores of print,
They await the coming bus.

   *   *   *

Slowly the boards rot and leach
Away in the subtle storm of time.
In the soughing, cords begin their screech,
Nails are rusted under the rime.

The will then lashes itself to the helm,
But the rudder jams and wheel fails.
The mast no longer holds its realm,
And now the lungs float out like sails.

And all is slow, still, and grave,
The cargo turned a sandy waste.
And what seemed once the dashing wave
Is but the shiftings of your dust.

   *   *   *

Yet tell me, how else, what else, shall
A prodigal crow fly out to see?
Being no more than a prodigal
Miser prodigal of misery.

Though foreign then, I kept the faith,
Pious still to the old ways;
Guided through the years by the wraith
Of chickens all those Fridays.

The ghosts began to trouble my soup.
Among the noodles, smoking breath
Stirred the cowardice in my cup.
Afraid to live, and afraid of death.

Afraid beneath the haunting cares
That rose to mock me with my fall,
Alone where the circle of my fears
Was bent like shadows by a wall.

Afraid of that predestined end
Toward which I saw the days crawl.
The wisdom a life had earned to spend,
Like shadows scattered on a wall.

And so I put by the things of man,
All became as one to me —
Packed in the absolute can,
Tinned into Eternity.

The lands I saw, conditions, men,
I thought unworthy of poetry.
Snob of the Absolute, in my pen
Blood turned the ink of mockery.

Death and myself were all I saw;
Between us desert and wrack spread far.
Beginning bad, the end a flaw:
A foolish thought, *mauvaise histoire.*

And then I saw the ark adrift
Under a sodden sky. I grinned
And thought, Return. Like a handkerchief
Its sail stood diapering the wind.

3. RETURN

Lullaby

For you alone under the eaves
At nightfall I sing these few black notes,
Which then become a sky and go like leaves
Under your lids, upon your throats —

For you alone. For you alone
My fretting wings trace in a little night,
The little night where all your years are one
And I am alone but for your light

To which I sing — for you alone.
I have come close again to watch your sleep;
Now that you are old and children of your son,
Slowly toward you my years creep. And I weep,

Under the eaves for you alone.

Arabian Night

This place, these women talking after dinner,
Before they rise to bless goodnight, I should
Know them, their stories of the past: sorrows,
Children, the dead; those very tales, yes!
Sisters, mother, aunt, still as they were,
Where the white table holds the dwindling room.
O genies of familiar memory, who,
Convened, becalmed, by nearness and the night,
Rub from a boy's fierce pride or impudence,
Or cousin's guile, or uncles' merriment
— So innocent, so unredeemed! —
A steady, timid spell against the night.

And I who sit like night at the window
And cannot enter except I become a child —
O that light has gone, they will not conjure him,
Not for all their burnished hearts' lamp!
He, in other lands, striving in chains, builds
But cannot grow; and I have come in his stead.
For here one is, Time's prosaic Sinbad
Returned from dull adventures in the years,
Ancient changeling, impostor of a life,
— His treasure, flotsam debased, befouled,
He cannot ransom forth the light, or save
This drifted past abandoned on a hill.

Become sole porter of my history,
What can I do but toss this black bag down,
Share the relics I've got, knock, return,
Like any prodigal — holding out
Tarnished gifts to strangers: some guilt,
Merely sentimental; a little childish loyalty;
A little useless pity.

Crystal

Be still! I have returned and turned to salt.
Is looking back the only guilt? on the city
In chains, the ark burst out like an apple.
And where are the seeds spilt?
The milk is turning, turning sour on the sill
This summer morning. And all is reverent, poised,
And still, idling, even as I, in the faulted crystal
Of the light; clear, beyond recall.
The steaming cornmeal, the table, coffee-mill,
The carrots sweetly burning, forlorn nail that waits . . .

Kernel of dawn, crystal of light held
Upon the eye like pale water flowing endlessly . . .
Until the eye fills — crystal
Where all is poised and still for a moment
Before it falls, as in a tear of salt.
Do they await my word to waken them to the fall?
Or do I cry because they are chained
In my guilt? I who am salt
On the dawn, a chain of wings upon the light.
The sleepers yawn. Even their faulted years
Seem a thing newborn and chill this morning.
Mama dozing with her bluest apron on
Dreaming she wears it to a ball,
And papa dreaming of his son . . .

And I of him this crystal morning.
Still! I have come home again. Be still,
I will cry crystals down to salt the wounds of time.
I alone have come back to know
And knock this morning at the door,
Yet they are still, as in a tear, as the sun
That fills the pale water, still as my laughter,
Dreaming they are whole.

Scratch . . . scratch. I come tapping the stone,
Blind remembering, blind with tears, scratching my grief
In the stone, blind wounds on the tomb of light.
Tap tap. And who will let me in? Shall
The crystal open, the ground awake, the dreamers rise?
I have scratched a mark this morning. Is there no seed
For its ground but broken timbers, littered stone?
I have brought a straw. But who will teach me to build?

III

III

WOMEN

(Mayagüez, Puerto Rico)

The rotted sun-weary shacks sit on the land,
Like a drowsy dog's tongue their doors hang idly out.
All around, the impatient weed and rutted clay;
Within, bare board, bed, table, chair. No more
Than this. No hearth, no picture, the window closed against
The sun. A baby weeps. The pot has business of its own.
And an aged woman retreats within the arms of a chair,
Her flesh thrown carelessly across her bones.

Her eyes wander through the dark to the empty wall,
To its broken altar where she has burned her hand, her thigh.
Flickering fingers recount her years in the wood,
And there she pours wine to her own sacrifice,
Kneels to the faceless board that devours . . .
And suddenly, quivering like an arrow, she is through —
Standing like Diana in the wood, and finds the leaf there,
The hound, the bow, an ancient mood of youth.

There the meadow and the spring, and there she hunts,
White and secret, through the bees and ivy. And finds
There forever her own body, whole, intact,
Like a sapling that holds still all its leaves,
As though inviolate and pure it hung the stars.
Now a wind blows and the door swings shut.

THE BURIAL OF A CHILD

(Bayamon, Puerto Rico)

Of an afternoon, sunny and still,
The mourners come with slow and lingering pace.
A dozen peasants climb the hill

Together, though alone. With grace
An uncle or father bears upon his head
The little lavender cask of his race.

Within, a child of two is dead.
And the coffin gaily limps like a boat at sea,
But lacks a flag. A child is dead.

And quietly they nod at me
And pass where an old stream had gone to rust.
Today a special dignity

Walks with each man through the dust:
They want to steal away this child from death.
And whatever they do this day is just.

And so their memories or breath,
Their sighs or smiles or secret crossroads rite
Dance around the lavender death,

Tiny waves that caress or bite
And take what is their due, dissolve the soul
With elements of the soul. It is right.

Of an afternoon, they talk and stroll,
And slowly so they struggle up the hill
And bring the coffin to a hole.

And how like a river they rise and spill,
Flow back upon the spring and goal.
A child is dead, alone, and still . . .

THOUGHTS OVER HERODOTUS

I

There are one hundred and eleven stations
On the Royal Highway of Darius
That runs between Sardis and Susa
Through a pleasant valley, rich, orderly,
And well-patrolled, and in each these houses
There is a strong guard and wine and a good bed,
Yet now must Asia, sprawled drunk with Xerxes' dream,
Spew along that gullet its lumps
Of flesh and rag that Athens' ranked oars
May chew them at Salamis.

That sunny day, Xerxes enthronèd sat,
A pine-bearing hill at his back
(And far away the beaten Hellespont
Whimpered and chafed at his pilings),
While, in the purple bay below, the ships,
Like leaves in the cup he stirred, swam and met.
He, from time to time, his golden spoon withdrew
And moved it through the air to nod upon
A ship; his scribes the hero's name did write
And the names of his fathers and his city's name.
The slow infusion of blood now began
To darken his perfumèd wine, and Xerxes' spoon
Showed red with rust against the pines.

II

Xerxes, colossal belch, shake Sardis
Till you leave it bald as a dandelion head
With all its seed swept at foreign wharves;
Bring up, Xerxes, on your father's road
The scalp-taking Skythians and the cannibals,
The father-eaters and flagellants,
The ear-clippers, tongue-clippers, breast-cutters,

Bring, Xerxes, the skin-strippers, the head-choppers,
The crucifiers, the blood-sippers,
Bring them, Xerxes, up the long road of the generations
That Athens may make marble of this mash,
And that this noble captain of the Skyth,
His long journey done, may dip the gilded skull
He carries, his drinking cup, deep
As the Aegean bottom to slake
His all-mastering thirst for death.

To flute and bell, in feathers and gold,
Moving as a dancer would who strove
Through air turned water, the endless host
Of Xerxes took one high step, their heads flew back,
And they gasped as men already lost.

III

This so Ionian skull, busy
With its thousand thoughts of enterprise,
O Onesilus!
Bees have hived in your head
And on your brow they track the rose,
The queenbee lolls on your tongue the day long
And bees spread honey through your curls.

Far from Cyprus and Amathus' walls
I set your honey-head in this still field
By the long road. Now may it be
To some their saltlick, to some their watertrough.

THE SYRACUSAN EXPEDITION

I

When the first ship cast its lines and slid away,
Someone struck a drum, then struck again;
Philo from his lyre shot arrows
Into every heart, and the crowds along
The wharves began their chant, commending Athens'
Fortunes to those departing. And then
The ships left one by one. Garlanded and drunk,
And light with song, the sailors let their long
Arms out and so caressed and stroked the water
That no salt broke from the violet swell.
Into his robes Apollo stepped and filled
The sails with his chest; long vistas hollowed
The deeps of his eyes, past and future whirled
In him like a wind. He blinks. But those who go
Forward looking back now make their oarlocks
Mew like gulls and toward Aegina fly.

II

A blankness falls on hearts, the dockmen pause
Among their half-coiled lines, the harbor stills;
Only — like nightbirds in the sun — orators
Grow shrill for the fading of their light.
The day's own glory has fallen on it
Like a sword cleaving the sultry morning,
Athens' rough block, wherein still coiled
An infant fate looks weakly out. The city
Cannot utter its hope and despair, they know
Their labor's borne this child and no other:
For every gain has its loss, and every
Loss its gain, yes, even for the same man;
For every chisel's stroke on stroke that bares
The god in the block destroys a different one,
Who falls to earth in the shard. And Apollo,
Piece by piece, gleams and goes out.

They stir, the thought of coming night revives:
The Bacchic dance, the petaled phallus, torchlight
Groping in the wine. They chant themselves home
By the long walls from Piraeus, and Bacchus
Draws a cloudy grapeskin over grey eyes.

III

That night the sailors bed their ships at Pylos
And gather at a fire, their chests yet rich
With the wine of beginnings. But the infant
Fate, already grown so tall, bends over
Cylon, the Chian archer, and strikes his face.

ADAM

Only light and shades of light
It was, and Eve a meaning there
Now water, now silver, now fire, now air.
Our senses then a slender height

That made sound silence, silence sight,
And this was light; the crystal throat of air
Drank the color from the flare.
But here is touch stupid as night.

Death has gathered in the twig
And hisses through his piercing thorn
The dappled leaf till now unseen,

And pours the olive, almond, and fig
From his swollen blinding horn.
All I know now is green.

NARCISSUS

I hear the great fish smack their tails
Upon the pane as they might flail
Their eggs into the mud; I see
The flat and the fat fish nose the glass
And turning in the water's pallid haze
Look up at me through my face.

Ancient ancestral arctic eyes!
Eyes immeasurably black, immeasurably cold.
So full, without desire, unsurprised,
And they unhungrily feed knowing all.
I am drawn to their pool
To find below my face my soul.

And what does it matter if all about
The bird sings on her egg and the frog
Croaks on its roe till it floats out
Among the reeds, if all the sunstruck bugs
Feast and chatter and the seeds swell
And the pollen lies thick as meal,

What if all is sun and song in the field,
If there's a humming and throbbing at the root
And all that busy life sings its clear note!
I know only those eyes that know all
Having coldly watched the ocean's dead
And the undoing of this world.

* * *

How beautiful my golden hair
Strung from the water to my head,
Strings of the lyre,
(Wind in the strings my voice)
And framed in the eyes' black, my face.
The eye grows wider till all is black;
I go among the dead.
What shall I find here? and what will appear
When I look back?

A POET

From earliest age he'd shown himself an adept of *décor*
And could not be anywhere long but he was on-stage
And obtrusively would produce from pockets a window, a door,
A table and chair, strike a pose, and say, 'This is Rage.'
And accompanied this attitude with prelude and postlude,
Or pointed heavenward to certain platonic flats
Awaiting their *entrée,* or seemed to engage a feud
With spirits under the floor, who were, in fact, under his hat.

I think he wanted to convince us our lives are papers
(Or that his was *not*) written over with the same old word
And folded up into gay little party favors
That go *pop!* and tell an ominous fortune if tugged too hard.
(It may be we *are* such miniscule literature.)
Articulate he was, but mistrusted eloquence,
For *that* pretends that something *is* real and, like Nature,
Can crumple one's performer's-smile with easy indifference.

An unpleasant shipwreck; though for this situation,
Too, he had a name somewhere in his everpresent valise.
For everything, he felt, was named already in the lexicon
Of public dreams — awkward, sad, and noble like his properties.
O perhaps he'd been a desolate child who'd murdered by fact,
Named his toys and thought them dead because respondent to his
No matter, for now he could be seen at the end of his act   [strings.
Grinning, grabbing up the tray, and scampering into the wings.

Well, and if he liked to pretend, at times, that the wind
He'd invoke to mow down a house of cards was *not* from his deck
And had not also, like all his gods, been machined,
Every magician believes that Chaos is the finest trick.
In his Master File of Forms, Norms, and Storms, he sought Repose.
But nameless death came and blew them all into a weather,
Deceived, deny it who will, by his Apocalypse-Pose.
It is to be doubted we live as well or die better.

A PAINTING

TO FRANK KUENSTLER

The distant, the official, vista has it so:
The horizon's grey barrier bands and halts the eye,
But thrusts from point to point a sudden spike of snow
That seems to rend the distant silence, and the sky.

And there is time in the long arcs that climb above your head,
So easy still to disband the mountain planes,
Open out the cones, and draw down the sky into the home of lead.
And yet, beholder, here you are in the foothills rattling chains.

How these grey rocks, like motes, cramp
The spirit! and climbing around, in, out, up,
Tires — yet the air is fresh, healthful the tramp,
The trees give out, but patience, courage, soon the top!

And there, O imagine it! we'll repay the eye's official call,
Gaze back, invent a dialectic, breathe, grin,
And watch the wheelings and gatherings-in of the Whole.
A spectacle unknown to man! — and sharpened by sitting on a pin.

A CURSE

If I forget thee not, New York,
May my ulcer of exile fork

Your sons, may impetigo and the yaws
Be on sale in all the stores;

May you like Chicagoans pronounce your r's,
May the handles fall from your doors

If I forget thee not; may your zippers stick
And drains plug, may you always eat at Nedicks;

May adultery be your only sweet,
No stain ever wash from a sheet;

May the theatres play one movie forever,
May the telephone ring never;

May the laundries take the buttons from your shirts
And the elastic rot on your skirts

If I forget thee not; may your letters be unsent,
May your Sunday dinners never end;

May the corks fall into the wine
And your fish be all scale or all spine;

May oil be found in Central Park,
May there be no place for cars to park;

May the ocean run from your taps
And Jersey claim you on all the maps;

May slugs jam every turnstile slot
If I forget thee not.

The good girls are down from the Bronx
Wearing ceramic jewels like a badge,
Whirling peasant skirts as they dance.
And the straighthaired blondes who busted college
Are carrying Proust around with Lawrence.
As I knew them

And the lost girls float with dark eye
And pale face, their diction studied, voices firm,
Like Cassandras crying, I will not cry!
The thin young girls have matronly arms,
And here and there walks a beauty.
As I knew them

And the Stalinists are there with guitars
And argyle socks, plaid shirts on their swelling chests,
Flogging the strings for the czar of czars,
The people; meanwhile their girlfriends' breasts
Are like brave new worlds, and simple as the stars.
As I knew them

Cooler than you, man, or I, the hipsters are cool
As the shining mountain stream at dawn
That trickles to its hidden crystal pool
Where the lapwing drinks, the hare, the fawn;
So cool are the hipsters, cooler, more cool.
As I knew them

The long white ones the sun has never seen,
Their eyes are like the earthsweated coal
Behind their sunglasses' evergreen,
Picking picking up the soul
With cocaine, heroin, and benzedrine.
As I knew them

Making it making it on manna are the shades,
Digging strange gods in the marijuana;
Today they're corn-fed Buddhas or de Sades,
Tomorrow Gnostics in the same old Nirvana;
Angular and drowsy in a world they've never made.
As I knew them

And the Bus. Ad. boys are down with their dates,
Callow faces poised like cream above their coffees.
The law students have mouths like revolving gates,
On their adam's apples, dazzling bowties
Gallop through blizzards of polka-dots.
As I knew them

And the fairies are out, dressed as queens
And princes; wads of cotton candy
Their little behinds in their tight blue jeans,
Like a terrible lollipop the head of one dandy.
And many are neo-Augustinians.
As I knew them

And the dykes are policing the johns,
They're cut in half by heavy belts, their necks
Are like clubs; but the voices of their minions
Are weak and strangled in their stomachs;
And small unshaven men are running their errands.
As I knew them

And the hoods with violet truncated faces
Like frost-bitten potatoes, and the lean
And crew-cut professional satyrs,
One with an Austrian voice like vaseline
Asking, 'Und vere are the Graces?'
As I knew them

The bald bachelors of forty are out, as always,
They go to bed with the morning papers,
Where all our lives are a little play;
Their weekend *Times* on cafeteria tables
Spreading its fatal wings over Sunday.
As I knew them

And the bums leak in from the Bowery
Like tiny black dust no sieve can catch.
Old Italians are silent in doorways,
They just happen to live here, and they scratch.
But the Olympians never come down from their parties.
As I knew them

Creep on, creeps! On Greenwich, on MacDougal,
Brothers, sisters, children mine!
So monstrous and so innocent all,
Because so young, and getting younger all the time.
— The Grace of Heaven is games in Hell.
As I knew them

In that glorious night our lives, my love,
Were like a marquee's blinking lights,
Blinking on and off. And did we ever move!
Seeming to dance out words all night,
Hand in hand now you now I going on and off.

THE TOURISTS IN SPAIN

Dizzy and light with hunger, we come
To greet the strangers by the side
Of the road which like a driver's whip
Dances down to us from Madrid and the North,
And drops biting the sea.

By what miracle do they come,
Shaking loose the light from their hair
And bringing sacks of corn and pearl
Out of the dripping Indies? Their bus
Gleams on the whip's black belly.

They arrive, they emerge, they walk among us
Tall as trees, pouring their buckets of shade
On our heads; they nod, and whisper
In the deep hollows of their mouths
Where spreading branches make a vault.

Such shoes they wear, heavy as saddles!
Such clothes, thick as cork between the fingers.
How must the wood be moist and warm within,
And their leaves turn ever to the sun!
The ladies' hats are pacing in the grass.

One bears an acre of grapes, they sprout
From the thousand vines of her veil.
The tendrils knot her ears and nose,
The small leaves flicker from her eyes.
O the many grapes rotting on her head!

The wind threshes the hats' straw, the wheat streams
Through town, a horse heavy as sand
Under each foot. It tramples ovens,
O wheat that walks my field in dunes!
Before me sails a hat, white and round

As the loaves of Tarragon. Three feathers
Say from its crown, 'Eat me, I am the bird
You ate last spring.' I run and take her hand.
We are two eagles rising from a feast
On the king's white flocks, mounting slowly till

We scent the wood-sweetened wind that blows
Off the mountains. I am an eagle of the Pyrênees.
I am ravenous, my beak curves, my claws
Flex. I fly down the wind straight to Madrid,
Straight to the Driver, screaming terrible cries.

Straight to his heart which I eat. The whip-hand
Goes slack, the whip runs off among hills.
I take him in my claws and beyond the land,
Beyond Cadiz and the Azores, and far over
The sea I fly feeding as I go.

BY THE SEINE

The uncommon glory of the day
Made me pause there on the *quai*
Where four old poplars stood,
Worthy to frame the greatest good,
And gaze across the even Seine
And all that tempered field of sun
As far as the Place Concorde.
So great the view, benign the air,
It seemed all mankind off the sword
Had slid like the water flowing there.

And then I saw a brazen plaque
Upon the promenade's low wall
That told how three soldiers fell
That very day some twelve years back.
On the walk before it lay
A disembodied red bouquet
Like an offering the wind had brought.
And *they* are roots without a plant, I thought,
And then, What a beautiful place to die!
And cried as anyone would cry.

THE HAND

I

Aboard a train three thousand miles
From whatever home I might call mine
I saw, across a valley of mortar and tiles,
The setting sun on a thousand windows shine
Till they were flames that woke and tossed
Like the thousand torches of a host
That marched in glory on the hill.
They marched, not I, I confess,
Stupid and dull with hopelessness.
Round and tart as an apple the wind fell,
The weather pursed and smelled of fall.

Then I remembered this was the day
When wine is lit in our feeble clay
And all who move find moving is to pray,
Who touch the world but touch in play.
For then the Torah is unwound, rewound,
To the fiddle's sound and foot's sound,
Rewound from that triumphant end,
Blest vision of the promised land,
Back to the bitter start
Where Creation cracks apart,
And then again begun.
But for this minute history's undone
And man is free, though through the long year
Week by week he give sweat and prayer
And never glimpse the promised shape.
Then, prophets riot in the grape,
And kings go dancing in the law,
Husbands leap, wives bring straw,
And greybeards stamp their feet for sign
As though to press the world to wine.
I, who was a child, would carry then
A tiny paper flag among the men,
A living apple crowned its wooden staff

And there a candle flared to laugh
Aloud the drunken mystery of night,
And made that dangerous glory a game
Where all that was not wine was flame.
I never knew, consumed in the ritual of light,
What the apple or the candle meant.

. . . So long ago, forgot when I went
Away. Nothing to mourn or repent;
Not lost, nor happy either.
The sun went down, the host under the hill.
And whether those symbols held a sweeter
Secret I was ignorant still.

II

Now must I in darkness turn,
Search for key and grope the latch
This umber hour of fall; and watch
The bats, and hear owls in the barren
Trees mourn. What curse has fallen? —
That I must sit in darkness sullen
Hour on hour by this stupid table
Counting down the minutes' babble
And cannot move, no, not for a match!
Was this the payment of my days?
I raised this hand to strike my flesh
— And saw it suddenly ablaze!
I saw my hand was light
Which all the blackened room made light.
The darkness was a sea of wine
Burning burning up the brine
Till the moment where I stood was bare,
And Canaan rising there.

'All that is not this burning hand,
Let it stand as wax may stand,
Run down or turn to smoke,
Be burning wine that it may raise
Up joy and hope in endless praise,
Though they be there to burn.
Let flame arise in the year's urn
Till all that dying is a brand,
Let fire on Canaan come, let it run
Laughing through the promised land
Till beginning and end are one,
Bound together on the fiery vine,
This burning evil, the other death.'

I moved this hand of mine,
I breathed, and this truth burned up my breath.

READING ROUSSET'S
'L'UNIVERS CONCENTRATIONNAIRE'

Who holds my book and turns the page?
Thinking of my brother Jews
I have crossed over the edge
And as one dead walk among the dead.
Who is it sits to read? —
Now that I wander like a shade
Bitter and free. Yet I who am ash
Fear they'll purge smoke as they did flesh
As even I forgot our death.
Who heaves my chest? who would draw my breath?

TO A THIRD-GENERATION ISRAELI GIRL

Anarchist or Socialist, I know not which,
Your grandfathers came to live on the soil
In communal freedom and by honest toil
A life orderly, strenuous, and rich,

You say, but sowed their corn to reap sticks:
For now these sheep the butcher did not kill
From camp and ghetto flock for no ideal
But their battered hides and bellies' politics.

O Batia, this irony's too great,
Nothing will contain it! madness sours
The earth, and furrows vomit seed and state,

These goads and palings, sterile monstrous flowers
Fraternity has borne. Yet once Israel knew
How father Jacob labored for his Ewe.*

* *Jacob was also named Israel; 'Rachel' is the Hebrew for 'ewe'.*

Higher into the half-light,
— While the children flow out
Of their shadows and the twilight

And, soaring and sinking, shout
To follow upward what they have sailed
Higher and slowly turning about, —

The great ball their breaths have swelled,
Purging desire with delight,
Is, like the whole soul healed,

There upon the summit of flight
Afloat, with no outline to break
It from the sky's descending light,

It also descending, to overtake
You in silhouette by the goal
You haunt and may not forsake,

While, over every bound, the ball
Grows downward from its height,
And sublime, continuous, and sole,

Enormous with all the suffusèd light,
Is here. Throw wide your arms,
You! embrace this world of light!

IV

THE FOUR

(After The Medici Tomb Figures of Michelangelo)

From that further place echoes
In confusion come; dull groans
That struggle on a buttress stone,
Sighs that pierce the darkness, gaspings, and
A fitful cough staggering on itself,
Then naked feet that shift along
The barren ground. And then no other sound
But labored breathing that grows calm,
Sobs that grip a heaving chest, that still.
I come upon that place. Open tombs
Let in darkness deeper than the night's;
Four figures on a pedestal take their dull
Repose, gathering what light the moon
Has left or coming sun disposes. And do not stir,
No wind stirs up their groans.

1. The Voices of Man

DAWN

Oh,   Oh,   Oh,   Why am I born?
Born to blindness bleeding light.
Why am I roused from desolation? —
Blind with night's black, blind
Staring in the sun, grieving what
I lost, what is to come; in this
Meager valley where shadows part,
Bringing light lacking eyes,
Eyes that grief has stunned.

Light, I rise in greyness, receding,
Damping, hollow, worn,
Like an eclipse of sun: I will not arrive.
O shadow from which I come, shadow
I cast, why do you drive me on?

DAY

This arm I am, this brutal crashing
Down of rays, this scourge and waste.
I am this hammer, making, breaking,
This hand you cannot stay, this face
Beyond a face. I am this flail,
This burden, this power to raise.
I am the pain in dying,
In labor I am the rage.

Will nothing exceed? Must the hammer stop
On the nail, nail in the springy wood?
I would build the endless tower, endlessly
Destroy it. But violence grows mad
Before this misery of flesh so quick devoured!
My body turns fleeing on the steps,
My head blazes over the brink
Staring in my fury's night.
O forms that die there, forms that grow,
Why do I build and blast?

What was I there? I remember,
I forget, in torpor sunk, in regret,
Hesitating, falling, on a breath.
What was I then? By what path
Did I come to sink sighing on this bed,
Heavy in the shallows of breath?
So useless is life, so useless death.
What was the past? Where was I then?
Gone in a breath, in the nagging mask
Of what I might have done. I cannot
Swallow more; murmuring self-murder,
Quarreling, gnawing my breath, my lip
This bloody bread, sinking in
Where all reliving's a death.

O night that lies in my steps, sleep
In my eyes, when will you let me rest?

NIGHT

With you I am falling
In the blackest rose where shadow-petal
On petal of shadow is laid, to deeper
Darkness leading, falling
Falling with you
And petal of madness on loss is lowered,
Lowers — I am with you falling
And denial sinks
On remorse, remorse falling,
And the forgotten hour is moist upon despair
And grey murmurers of limit are descending,
Descending and falling, in armies of wings
Dropping, and absence swallows out the light
Falling with you
In the heart of dying
The blackest center of blackest rose:
Sleeping I am with you
In perpetual falling poised —

For my eye is on the flame.
I am its gathered darkness, the world is
Exceeding light, and light of light,
And of that light still light, and yet
Is light unloosed and light unending!

And I ride out with you along the riverside,
In the damp marsh I hold the horse,
Speaking in your ear my news
Of the journey, I am your frosty
Breathing, the ground of your walking,
The listening companion, now a bridge
And now an abyss; like the winter's sun
I move with you, in the crackling forest,
Where the white birds sing.

GOYA

1. Man

The soldiers bear a sack,
A white sack without a tear;
The soldiers are in black.
For the rest, the plain is bare.
And what else *should* be there?

They carry the sack,
They do the best they can;
One in his arms, other on his back.
Are these animals that feed on bran?
No. They are men. This is a man.

2. 'Se aprovechan'

'They take advantage' — the soldiers need clothes,
While the corpses don't, who have their repose
And nakedness like a second birth,
And nose-down sniff new science from the earth.
So what if nakedness admits the crows!

Such handsome athletic figures,
Twenty centuries of nudes! which now the soldiers
Like bungling apprentices of the muse
Or drunken helpers in a museum cellar,
Yank and tug at to uncover.

And doing so, give that hopeless bric-a-brac
A little of the rhetoric of passion back.
Behind, a giant tree with haunches of a mother,
In her anguish torn and flowering and black,
Rears up! — but her head is out of the picture.

3. Other Mutilations: Disasters of the Deaf

No, not the sound — that's not his — they steal
The silence, their machines have sucked the space
Out through his ears, *his* space, *his* silence, unloosed
The inner volumes of his body; hopeless to feel
Within himself, and in a place.

And the eye reposeless; here surfaces crack,
And his eye bewildered, weighted with trying to hear,
Aghast, in the ragged depths, before the huge dim spook
Of skin and stones, the *them!* the horror: the hacked
Cadaver of his space. But right, or left, a path there

Winds away, out of the present, into a nowhere
That's gone, a something or nothing, all white or all black,
Not his or theirs! — but a *path,* escape! like an inward ear.

4. The Duelists

We look at masker, mask, and think: tree/root,
Face/soul. A pretty word-game wherewith
The world's made one; which these masks refute,
Saying: white/black — surface of no depth,
Depth without surface, as: bare foot/empty boot.

See, the darkness fills an eye or stains
Across a mouth, and their swordpoints daze the air
Like black flies buzzing here/there
That light and leave and touch, as on two windowpanes,
To learn what world of blackness a little mask contains.

5. The Nightmares

O Beauty! O . . . but that no longer twists.
Better these after all harmless succubi
With noses you can grip with both fists,
And dwarfs with humps like a witch's saddle,
Outrageous hairy runts who come knee-high,
And No-faces sketched in on a paddle,
And Hot-feet who jump up and down, hop hop,
And cackle and cry and bite their hands, and stop.

Little children, in fact. O may they now come
Unto us, bringing their tantrums of delight;
O, in this banal twilit delirium,
May these idioms, crotchets, slips of the brush
Come daub their mimicries of our human fright.
Well then, is it asking too much
To have, before the frozen night of terrors,
Such charming playmates as these lively errors?

6. Saturn

Is it ambition leads him there?
The witty artist starts in air —
Where exclusion, balance, order disclose
An ethereal and delicious pose,
And intimate a phantom doggie and
Two subtle feet that stray or stand
Beneath the portrait of a doll.
An art of seeming not to fall.

But hunger brings one back to earth:
To carnival maskers, madmen, clowns,
Dark hordes of cobbleheaded crones,
— The riotous fictions of rebirth —

And odd bones the war has left around;
So much to feed those starving wits,
To be gotten down. But somewhere's a ditch
Of blackness always dropping underground

— To where the monster, lit by a chthonic glow
And having eaten the charming *cogito*,
Now lifts a bloody torso like a toy,
As if, poor thing, there was only one joy;
At the bottom of all, this preposterous end
That wit cannot define or passion comprehend.
And the black holes in the fiercely rounded whites . . .
But be careful! don't touch it! — it bites.

THE GNOME

1. My House

Wind in a poor man's drain
Rattles like a dying mute.
But I keep snug all year long,
Keeping house in a buried boot.

Bed I have, and stove and pot,
And do the things I please.
I watch the clouds go by like kings
All kneeling to the breeze.

2. My Occupations

I have counted seams in my coat,
Those in coats of the poor.
So many there as when the wind
Blows stars through a broken door.

Tick-tack the tailor goes,
And here's another star!
So hearts are held together.
Tick-tack, the needle's never far.

3. How I Live

They come to me, they say,
Wise man, tell us how you live.
O I would answer, Like the tree.
I take nourishment and thrive.

With what wry complement of tones
I and the soaring poplar say,
I couldn't live as I do
If I didn't do it every day!

4. Who I Am

'Who are you?' by ants, worms, and other
Of my devoted I'm asked *ad infinitum*.
'He alone,' I say, 'in all this world
Who could bear to be the being I am.'

Which definition I proffer one and all
As being true — though, maybe, I fear,
More than lovers, easy under
Each other's burdens, can safely bear.

5. My Doorway

When tired of this heavy world,
I lift the door and step outside
And look up at all that emptiness
Long ago leaked from my side.

All night, all day, I see
The sun abandon,
The moon abandon,
The stars go off.

6. *My Neighbors*

Some walk, some run,
But all agree the road is sure.
Underfoot they cannot feel
The sorry stones' discomfiture.

They know not what I have seen
Under the hurrying rout
— The long sleepers stretched there,
Their long tongues sticking out.

7. *Visitors*

All on the road go grim or slack,
Eyes to earth or eyes to the poles.
None could guess from how they walk
The bitter tickling of their soles.

Their shoes bear little faces
Which eat the dust with grins of a clown.
Let them walk to their ankle-bones,
They will not wear them down.

8. *Other Occupations*

It's I who light the will-o'-the-wisp,
I lay their bed of grass.
The lovers think the fire they draw
Will linger when they pass.

Or think because they hold so tight
They have the thing they hold.
Yet they have passed away to seek
Where all their earth has rolled.

9. *How I Solve Problems*

Who am I? What's the world?
Wherever I look I see my nose.
It stands like a lonely rock
Receiving the cold wind's blows.

Heart, take ease! I yet will know
The name and being of the One.
It gathers in the hollow place
The wind begets in stone.

My Favorite Flower Is: the Red Rose.
My Favorite Occupation Is: Repose.
My Favorite Game: Articulation.
My Favorite Fear: Suffocation.
When I Grow Up I Want To Be: the Same,
Only endlessly and more fascinatingly more so!
My Favorite Element Is: Earth.
My Ultimate Aim
Is (without further ado):
Rebirth.

THE WANDERING JEW

O Jerusalem, if I forget thee, may I die!
If I forget thee not, how will I live!

1.   The Gates of Gaza

I, sidelong in this obscene world going,
Under battery of filth, bawdry of elements,
Perjurious day forsworn and grieving
At night's bar, all loud and absurd,
Absurd and foul, in this butchery
Of flesh, carnival of fur, I
Running, and on my back the Gates
Of Gaza from the world's muck pulled
Like a rotten tooth — to be carried where?

Never to rest, never to sink down at road's end,
Knowing the journey over, the thing done;
Never to reach settled city, never come home,
By every road withdrawing from that;
Never to rest, accounting this taint of
The soul's honor, debasement of its gold;
Never to sleep, never to know long rhythms
Of earth, the water slowly moving, a light.

O Jerusalem, where shall I build thee? What hill
Is high enough? what earth so rich? what people
Good? Where shall I set down the Gates?
Having no city but this heart of weed and cloud,
Trampled and foraged by herd of folly,
By brutal bodies' violent milling there.
Ridden by goodness I go,
God, in the damp mist descending,
Running at my ankles like a dog.
Why for the pure task these tools of dirt?
This abstracted heart, this fever, this world?

2. The Face of God

Upon the altar of the kitchen stove,
Enameled white and shining with the cares
Of hands that giving, graced with love
Three meals a day for thirty years —

There at Friday dusk it crouched beside
The weekend's pit, the mount of Sabbath:
A tumbler-candle dimly hissed and sighed,
Too sweet to judge, too nice for wrath.

All night long the wax ran down
— Crying dead to whom we burnt that rod.
They in the ghostly tallow lay to drown
The bent body of the dying god

Who lit a platter-clock that ticked our sleep.
Its even hands dipped in the dark streaming
And up and down carried us in their sweep.
Chests rose and fell like empires dreaming.

And now I wander accused by that Sinai
In a glass, by muteness of our closet wish,
By a God humble, tiny, and good. And I
Choke with pathos of a clean dish.

O God, in my exile and affliction hear me!

From my enemies, save me! Scourge, burn, hash,
Make their inner rot grow badges on their flesh!
Why did You tempt me with goodness? why do You crease
With pain? why this suffering that won't cease?

Here am I stupidly living in sackcloth and ash.
Why was I born just a year before the Crash?
Why'd my father lose his lots and his cash
And go jobless till a gentle lack of courage
Was inbred? Then why'd I grow in this image?
How can I be a hero if I'm not half a fake
Like my cousins Joe and Jake?
To be Chosen — that means having only one part.
But if I'm Elect, why all this fat around my heart?
Why was I born in Brooklyn in the lower middle-classes?
Is that a hero's place? Was Moses freckled! Samson wear glasses!
Why me? Haven't You had F. D. R. and Cecil de Mille?
(Pardon me, O Lord, if I question Your will,
But wouldn't Seymour or Sherman have done as well?)
Why do You tell me to build when I want to destroy?
Can't a Jew get that job, is it only for a goy?
Can't a Jew be bad and mean, why sad and nice?
Do You think it's better to have ulcers than a vice?
Why, when I damn others, must I look for my own guilt?
If the evil aren't all bad, the good all good, can't I cry, Tilt!
Couldn't You've come as an angel, not a pebble in my shoe?
When I crashed Katz's car did he have to sue?
And then in court, why didn't You put in Your Word?

Don't I know what Sisyphus doesn't, that only pain's absurd?
Then why don't You teach me to strike and not to complain?
Why do You let me suffer if it's not to suffer better again?
Isn't my hardship bitter? my pain pain?
Why did You send that fat bureaucrat against me?
And that spiteful sage and that selfish landlady?
Why, if You love me, didn't You strike them down?
Bend closer, my God, I can complain till all the stars drown.

4. Assimilation

I dreamt the other night I was in Heaven,
That I rose up like a sundae with leaven.
I was there in the Old Folks Home playing pinochle and checkers
And up above us is a picture of Old Abe who fried the neggers.
Everything is free and grade-A. Then I turn over my card.
It says, 'What's good for Ford is good for God.'
And all the boys are gathered sitting around the Televidge,
Clear as day you can see God's own image.
He talks sweet and low and he looks like Ed Murrow,
The music's by Gilbert and Ed Sullivan; then it all goes blurro.
And Maxie whispers, 'He's Self-Sponsored, Self-Applauded, Self-
        Rated,
One and Almighty. It's a quality show and never outdated.'
'Haha,' I say, 'boy, that's rich!'
'Shhh,' says Bennie, 'He owns half of Miami Bich.'
But I figure I'll unload 'cause the market looks too bullish.
But Barney whispers, 'Don't do nothing fullish!'
So I hang on and buy till the ticker goes screwy
And I'm 10 million bucks ahead and the bears are all blooey.
The sky's full of stars going around in their tracks like at
        Graumans Chinese,
And they start handing out autographed menus from Lindys,
The guys're all drunk and there are B-girls and bagels
And free silver dollars straight from Las Vegals
And Bella grabbed me and said, 'Hey, we're all angels!'
But I'm worried, why does Mr. Mortie have to run after the
        models?
Can't he stick to his dressmaker's dummy and keep out of the
        Catskills?
That buyer from Phillie! That union contract! O, I wanna scream,
        Halp!
Seventh Avenue's waiting for my scalp.
But Gimbels takes a thousand and Macys takes ten and then it's
        bam!
And I buy Rausye a mink for her old persian lamb.
And Grossingers was giving a banquet at Woolwoits
And Sollie was laughing it up trying on the skoits,

And Albie said, 'Moishie's under the Boardwalk gettin' laid.'
And Sadie said, 'Come on, let's go sit in the shade.'
And Marvin sank a heaver and Joey hooked from the side,
Then Creepie drove in for a lay-up while the other guys cried.
And Bernie pulled a mouse-trap and Skinnie's pass hit the mark,
And forever and ever the Mighty Babe stood swattling 'em outta
    the park.
Then after the spelling-bee we have a map-drawing contest
Of the United States and teacher says mine's the best.
But Sidney and me, we snuck into the Loews
And this guy sits down and starts tickling our knees.
And I say, 'Leave us alone, mister,' and he says, 'Say please.'
And then he says, 'Wanna see the scar under my kiltie?'
And I look and o my god it's uncle Miltie!
And they all think the Lone Ranger is really a crook,
And on the street papa says hello to Mr. Bashook.
Then the kids all pile in and we start throwing rocks.
On the radio Uncle Moe says, 'Irving, there's a present in the
    icebox.'
O god, I feel all soft and I wanna cry and twitch.
There's a card, it says, 'For your throat, a thirty-year itch.'
And there's a can the size of a man, and mama's in it!
'Mama,' I cry, 'I found you again!' 'Don't talk,' says she, 'itt!'
And I'm standing in my crib and I say, 'Papa, buy me a tri-cycle.'
And he spreads his wings and smiles like the American Ikele.
And it's always dark and everything's free and you never hear
    No.
But I can't breathe and think I'll drown in the stuff and nobody'll
    know.
And I wake up kicking and screaming, Lemme go! Lemme go!

5. Scratch

If I must stay where I am, my God,
How will I survive on this patch?
God said, Scratch

And if I'm so sick of this world
Its mere thought makes me retch?
God said, Scretch

But what shall I do, my God,
To cure me of this Heavenly itch?
God said, Scritch

And if Your time be here, how will
I know, having lost my watch?
God said, Scrotch

And if the Messiah comes today,
How, my God, will I get in touch?
God said, Scrutch

But if I must go speak Your Word,
Where will I say it? to whom preach?
God said, Screetch

And though I sweat and struggle, what if
The Devil puts me in his pouch?
God said, Scrautch

But if he bears me off with him,
How will I find You, how approach?
God said, Scroatch

And if, my God, Your door be locked,
And I cannot cannot lift the latch?
God said, Scratch

O, where are You? Your voice like
A record worn, only one word I catch!...
Scratch, God said, Scratch

V

DYING

(Prometheus)

1. Revelation *(A negative)*

Time of the blinking of an eye. So quick.
And this was revelation: Man Is Here —
This single signpost where all roads arrive,
Depart, like dusty twinkling messengers
The mountains could not hold. And then are gone —
While my hands lift upward to the sky this world,
Whose sun is blackest of all, all intensities
Of sight with soot dimmed, dirtying the air;
While, from beyond, weak light drifts through
Like birdsong on the empty roads. Indeed,
It was morning — from the white shadows arose
A little wind scuffing the dust and mist
Of light which had been man, and drove it sighing
Up the valley into the hills' gold shallows.
Man was here, had built: the temple, the house,
The tomb, the furrow — all darkened now
Where the sun struck, or lay speaking to itself.
Around all simple things, handles, knobs,
A broken tree, the shadows were a blank
Of space, where the sun in purity fell through.
And I yawned, greeting that bright and dark day;
Man was here, still laboring in my thumb's prize,
I yawned, and could not breathe, smoke
Fell in my lungs till I thought I would die.

2. Breath (A phantom dialogue)

I

Can I recall the tree, the temple of breathing?
Where four great branches spring upward from the trunk,
There is a hollow cup, mysterious and plain,
Whose emptiness informs the limbs,
Their overflowing dialogue of changes.

Where will I find the space, the breath, the breathing?
Where? But where is the cup? Here,
Dead center of the wide world,
The instants are a breath apart,
Specks of light scattered through a stone;
And freezing wind comes and goes,
Shaking the grizzled twilight
Till the granite leaves are shaken down;
Their voices cry aloud with mine, 'Who are you
Beside me, calling? what echo of myself?'

Out of the dust they cried, and dying called,
'You, did you hear me? did you answer?
Are you there, beside me?
I cry, I call. Creature! Where is the wind?'

II

How will you know your chest from the night?
— When the sphinx has come, to crouch there asking
Its inexorable question. How will you raise it up?
How will you call? The night is here, asking
'Where are you? You, where are you?'
How will you inform the night?
Blackness annihilates the depths,
Roads vanish in the monolithic plain.
How will you say, 'I am here. Here I am?'
Breath is a question, breath the answer.

But when your heart's hammerstrokes
Stutter, I, I, I am,
And your voice calls out, 'Where are you?'
You!
How will you know yourself from the night?

3. *Hand*

The hand made: All,
Which is the motion of a breath,
Rising falling,
Of one breath in one moment,
Moving from horizon to horizon,
Which is the form of breath,
Of one breath, this home.

In the moment of dying without breath,
The hand said, All,
Building a primal space, a world
And its roundness, as an exhalation does;
And sought to gather the horizon back,
And vaguely, here and there, to point, to touch,
To take the things out there, each one sealed
In its rotting space, where a dawn fell through.
In the moment of dying without breath
The hand said All, trying
To build a breath.

At dawn the butterfly hoists its little sail
And steers out, and white wing down, wing up,
Pieces together grass and sky, sky,
Sky and earth; so the hand, moving
Toward the past, the last horizon,
In a wilderness of wind,
Searching for a breath in the wind,
In the moment of dying
When the horizons draw apart
And there is no place under the sun.

The leaf retreats in the stem's throat, the tree,
Choking, re-enters the seed, seed flies up.

No breath is in the wind,
This flowing of the space of things
That no longer are, blooms
Of hollowness rushing away,
Bursting together like bubbles.
Breathless space of a camera box.
The seeking hand retreats
With the winding up of time,
An image in a reel reversed
That finds itself, staggering back
Toward its own first figure:
Mute fist of motions unmoving,
Aimless thing the wilderness
Disposes, destroys
In the moment of dying
This homeless home
Breath of no breath.

4. The Beggars of the Source

I

Who ask and do not want,
Receive, and do not live,
Are they not ranged beyond
The saints of abnegation, who wanted
And did not ask, forgave
And did not die? Waking,
Are they not greeted by infinities blown
From the negative norths of life, withering
The morning mist on the boughs of things?
— Till trees stand
In the clear winter without paradox,
Facing into a blueness of eyes.

They stare, and commonest things appear, you
Appear, as legions, infinitudes: hammer, torch, cloud
In columns standing to the horizon.
Then how can your hands' crazed gesture,
Building or giving or taking,
Arrive at the hopeless recession of their being?
— You who stand bare, contending,
Particular, like a strangled tree
The horizon cannot cope.

(And dream; but is it dreaming
If surfaces appear? this violent calm
Of things that, undesired, stand amazed:
Astonished glass, sugar squared
In dense surprise on a golden cloth;
Or, marbled with absence, a loaf —
Like a bright salvo — thunders in their heads!)

II

Here in this spot where the river stirs,
The river or their hands; here, like Fates
The caving horses of the wind have dropped
At dusk beside the dusty sycamore
And iron bridge where the narrow river starts
Bearing down a fireless winter sky,
Here on a stone they sit, sunk like knots
In the cosmos of their coats, inert as a point,
Still as horses sleeping.

Here is the source,
Where, its element gone by, desire gasps,
And beggar from his hopeless heart
Pays: lean stone, lean air, lean water.
Nameless, unnaming, nightlong making
Change to dust, of movement a space, all day
With aimless mill of hands spinning water
From a rock; mouths that do not drink, eyes
That stare, like pure directions, from nothing
Into nothingness.

And here the source.
Prometheus went under their hands.
His form trickled through the rocks; utter blackness
Of fire; his shadow a mist upon the trees.
Night. And never. Nowhere.

BIRTH

(Theseus)

1. The Monster

You inevitably: there, before the world's
Beginning, waiting, watchful, hidden in a block;
Or after the world's ending, there, inevitably,
Like a universal scabbarded in stone.
You, self-reliant, identical, redundant,
In the dark spaces
Before the first flaming of terror, after its expiration.

Inexhaustible from dark sticks
The dance and dancers come,
I come, gorgeous in flame,
Lifting my flourishing wrist,
Abounding rich decoration
And this my playful laughing lust,
One ripening moment that must
In a moment be gone.
Eight-armed I am, I glide
Reaching my multitudinous hand;
I am shape of movement satisfied,
Within the burning matter stand
Raising limb's joy from wood's desire.
Then, if limb and limb conspire,
I grow one body of delight
And new limbs embracing the new night.

It is you: in a black vizor, behind a pillar,
Gazing, marking time, the fiery intervals
You cannot see because there you are, minding
Your business with paranoid intensity,
And, suddenly, you stand beside yourself,
In a black vizor, flashing signals.
And your laughter detaches, whirls up jangling,
For you are blind harlequin daydreaming

Of the day, your choicest rôles! — Victor, Victim,
Avenger — a king within the costume,
Where you are yourself, you, unchanged,
Your lineament transmuting every mask,
Like the one figure among a window's
Shifting lozenges; and, neatly contained
By each outline, you are tinkling together
— Such freedom you have,
These mimings of a bound man
Freely falling,
One groundless moment,
Through a breath.

Night within the leaf, night
Of the twig, the stone's night, the flower's
Are flames in these my easy powers
Flowing upward into light.
All things, their nights that yearned
To grow now free now luminous
Exchange their selves across my caress;
I am them all, eternally returned
Out of the burning wood, a tree of all delight
Rising in destruction.
When my ripening moment's gone
I hang the ripened nothing of the night.

A moment before, wielding your sword, you
Were there, elsewhere, nowhere.
And here, in a stillborn silence, this moment,
The slate is clean: blackness, and again nothing.
And your whim darts out, in bounding strokes,
Drawing from the treadmill of the moment,
Between parentheses, the labyrinth,
Saying, Let this be elsewhere, and elsewhere.
Expanding, running on, gigantic: elsewhere out
Of elsewhere. And nothing. You,

In a little blue absolute, between parentheses:
A god. And your laughter, flapping elbows,
Scrawls its infinite articulations,
And hovers and mourns the dead disguises,
And goes gaily forth bearing new impasses
To new elsewheres; while you, drawn apart
And circumspect, in appropriate garb, elsewhere,
In another moment, look out upon the dark
And say, It was good. Falling asleep

In the womb of the Minotaur
Whose breath from every pore
Flows upward into flame
That, leaping in the dance,
Flame and flame shall recommence.

2. *The Animal*

1. DAWN

Something was slain.
                          Desire, which no image
Can enclose, overflows in flame
On dancing flame — and the dream flows after,
Brazier into bird, the burning room

Rising in fire; here, always desire
Is here before the lagging figures
Which cannot contain, cannot capture,
Through all their voluptuous changes,

Burning and born, this fire; and they, too,
Are fluttering with desire, form dying
In form in heart of fire, till the image

Vanishes in light, this world of light,
Here, rousing the dreamer to the place
Desire has shaped. But birdsong, this

Piercing delight. It is the dawn.

He wakes to light, where his body is light,
And feels his strongly tautening skin,
And corresponding nakedness of light
No costumery of hope may mask.

This is the one, the heart's own dawn!
The body thrills to self-possession,
And knows itself, and knows it is fulfilled
As flesh, this selfless light wherein,

Surpassingly new, surpassingly familiar,
So quickened by the body's desire,
All things become this second body

Singing, 'We could not be were you not here,
You could not be elsewhere.' And beckon him,
Who is always at home, always in love,

To rise to them from the glowing floor.

This thread is the way of his going,
A sinew that is no object's bound
Yet has composed the world with its flowing,
— As if his body's outline were unwound

In one continuous moving dance
That cannot pause upon a single figure
But still escapes from every stance
In harmonious gesture after gesture

That rise from their dialogue with the ground,
Become the rhythmic living place.
Moving is such grace.

Yet he goes toward the cave's bright round
Transfigured by a companion death,
This hardness underlying all ways.

And now he stops, and draws a first breath.

3. Man

1.

Something was slain.
　　　　　Indeed, 'something' was 'slain'.
Words are easy. But life is hard. Death
Is harder still. 'Still.' That's a word.
Well, and now to set the scene: *Before a cave*
Whose black mouth to one side is visible,
In a hollow cup, some natural and modest
Amphitheatre, in whose midst a tree
Is presently to spring (only later,
When appropriate), *enter* solus, *running*
From the cave, I, looking wildly out,
Addressing everyone in general
And no one in particular,
For so it is I want it done:

Death is the hard thing. To be here in
A bloody clout and alien pelt
And smell the rank animal I've killed,
Not killed, murdered! and feel the broken fur
Still starting with terror of the knife,
And the last caress of the animal-
Mother when she sent me out. And then, *not*
To gasp aloud the horror! Is it easy
To be born and not vomit? to spring
From murder to this haunted
Babble on a stage? And then to stare
Through eyes of a dying animal into
Fire or a knife, and wear foreign flesh
Whose reek of matted blood must year by year
With the body's slow degradation grow
Uncannily my own, this hairshirt, shirt
Of Nessus, this one disguise you must become,
Sentenced to die for the guilt of being born!

2.

I had prepared all manner of conceit
And splendid metaphor, images both
Natural and rare, to show how dancing's done,
And show we're always Nature's, that if only
We can praise the moment and what is given
In it, even ourselves dying, then must
We move by our heart's desire and all
Its blest fatalities, and, living that
Perfected hope, the sense of oneself moving,
Cannot misstep, if only we hallow
And will not violate.
                        But under
The circumstances, how could this be song?

This hard thing. This resists. I can
Rest my foot on it. Therefore, can walk,
Therefore, can feel this resonance, my voice,
Exciting the full flesh. I am not
A throatless ghost. I am here. I sing.
Yes, I shall learn this, hold to this way,
My dying. I shall hallow the ground,
My mother earth, who set me in this flesh
And bid me dance and sing.

And just to sing, and feel the song,
What sweetness strikes the tongue,
Fulfills the heart with richness as with flame!
Here in this lingering descant of the scene
To speak the things as they'd be spoken,
Naming cave, blood, tree, hollow,
And feel the dwelling note and word
Become the song's enchanted place,
Where they in steady sweet procession
And this my discipline of dying
May loosen to the splendid dance.

3.

Whom this quick bolt touches
Is shaken so with dread
He knows the living terror
And cannot know death:

When, in a circle of trees,
A leaf curvets and falls,
Fierce spines of attention
Spring suddenly from its dark
Downward path, startling
Life to the given space,
And are a tree arising,
Column vivid and pure!

THE LOST LANGUAGE

I have eaten all my words,
And still I am not satisfied!
Fourteen thousand and twenty blackbirds
Hushed under my side.

And when I think of what I have written
Or might have and can and shall write
— My life, this appetite,
But how shall I eat the food forgotten?
And think of how my envy like a lust
Kept me up all night with its tease,
And how the night unveiled a noble bust
When I thought of glory — but that doesn't please.
So much ambition,
And so little nutrition.

Après le déluge, moi.
There it is, all the sad tale —
A perfect post-diluvian male,
And other humanist ta ran ta ra.
For, after all, it's only disgrace,
At the very best, to outlive
(Half-monadnock, half-sieve)
The saddest thing in the life of the race.

And when I think how many fathoms deep
Debris of that mighty birth ...
O then there were words in the earth!
That were the things they named
And lay like manna in easy reach,
And when you spoke, there was speech.

Very hungry and not a little ashamed,
For passion is no longer food,
I have taken up again,
In ghostly parody, pot and pen,
And sit to gnaw my chattering brood.

One cup of Lethe and it's always too late.
Where are you, *o liebe breyt*? *

* *Yiddish for 'bread'.*